THE BEATLES

The NEXT THREE albums from the original British collection.

Arranged by TODD LOWRY

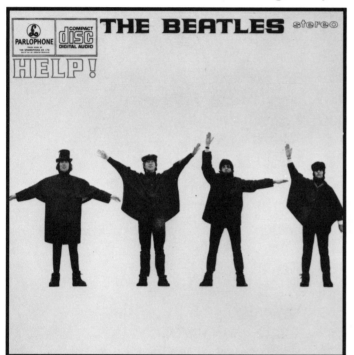

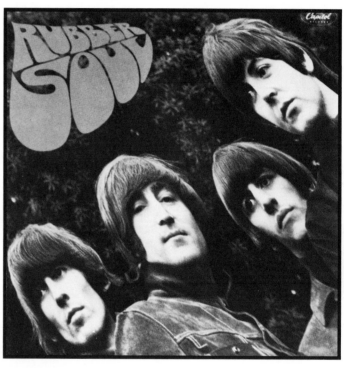

This publication contains songs made famous by The Beatles.
The Beatles are not connected in any way with Northern Songs or its licensees.

HAL LEONARD PUBLISHING CORPORATION

Home Office: National Sales Office:
960 East Mark Street   8112 West Bluemound Road
Winona MN 55987   Milwaukee WI 53213

Index of Songs
ALPHABETICALLY

THE
BEATLES – the NEXT THREE albums

Index of Songs
BY ALBUM

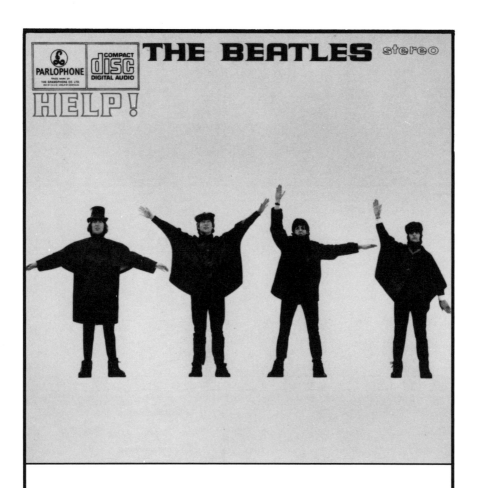

HELP!

Moderately, with a driving beat

Words and Music by
JOHN LENNON and PAUL McCARTNEY

Help! I need some-bod-y, Help! Not just an-y-bod-y, Help! You know I need some-one, ___ Help! ___

Now I find   I've changed my mind,   I've o - pened   up the doors.
I know that I   just need you like   I've nev - er   done be - fore.

Help me   if you   can,   I'm feel - ing

down,   And I do   ap - pre - ci - ate

you   be - ing   'round.

THE NIGHT BEFORE

Words and Music by
JOHN LENNON and PAUL McCARTNEY

1. We said our ____ good - ing
2. Were you tell - ing

byes, ____
lies? ____

Like the night be - fore.____

ANOTHER GIRL

Words and Music by
JOHN LENNON and PAUL McCARTNEY

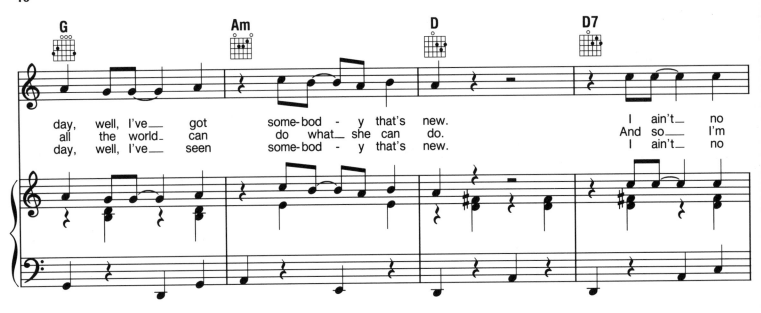

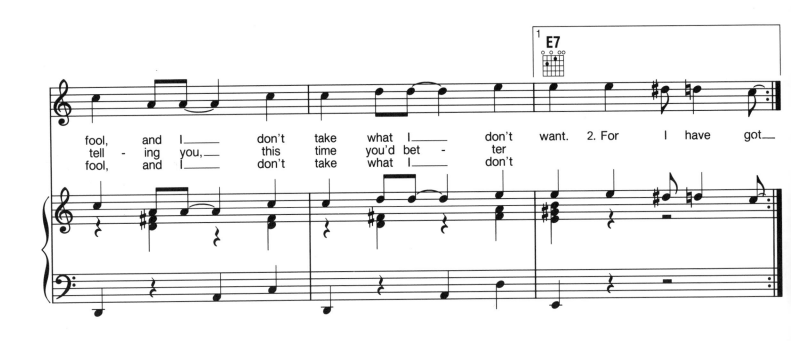

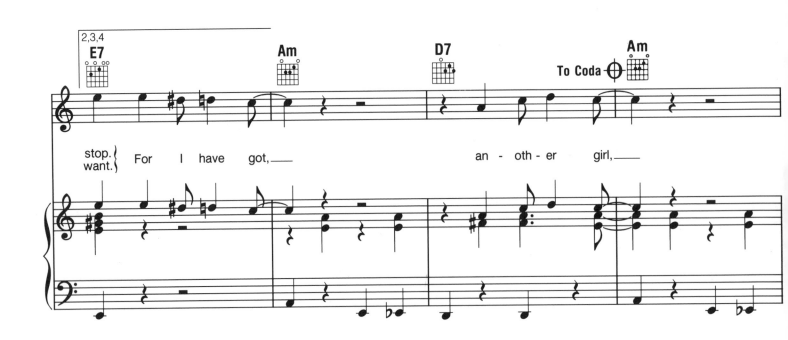

YOU'VE GOT TO HIDE YOUR LOVE AWAY

Words and Music by
JOHN LENNON and PAUL McCARTNEY

I NEED YOU

Words and Music by
GEORGE HARRISON

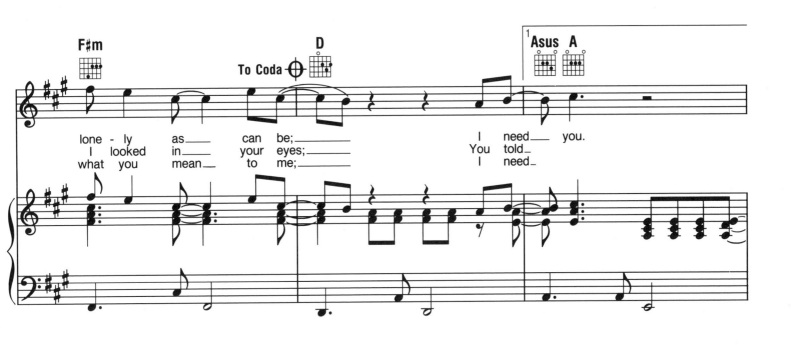

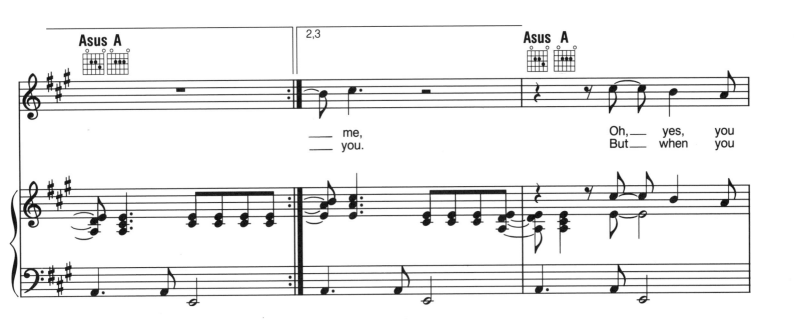

told me   you don't want my lov-in' an-y-more.___
told me   you don't want my lov-in' an-y-more.___

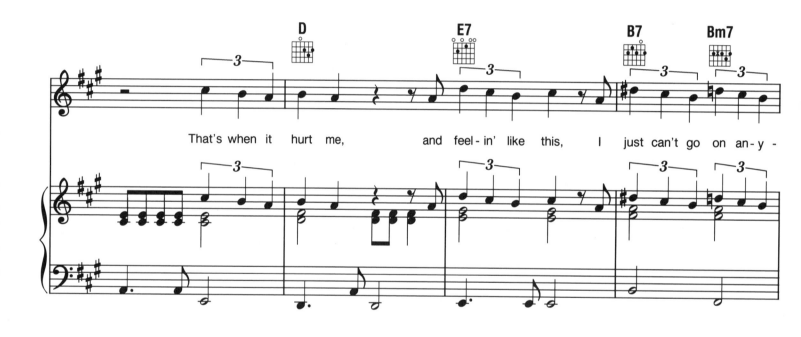

That's when it hurt me,   and feel-in' like this,   I just can't go on an-y-

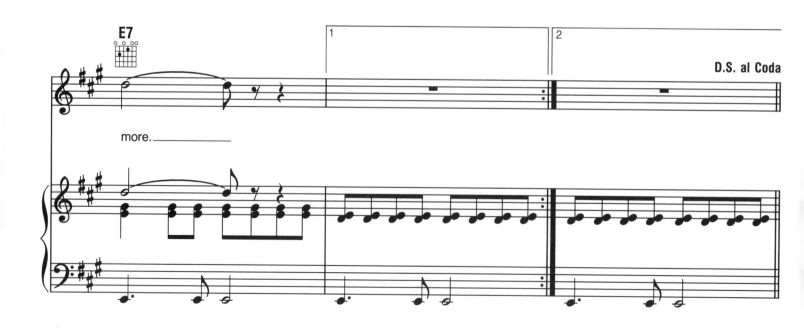

more.___

D.S. al Coda

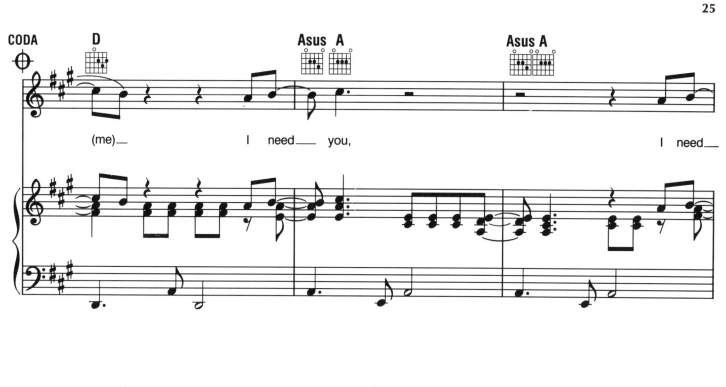

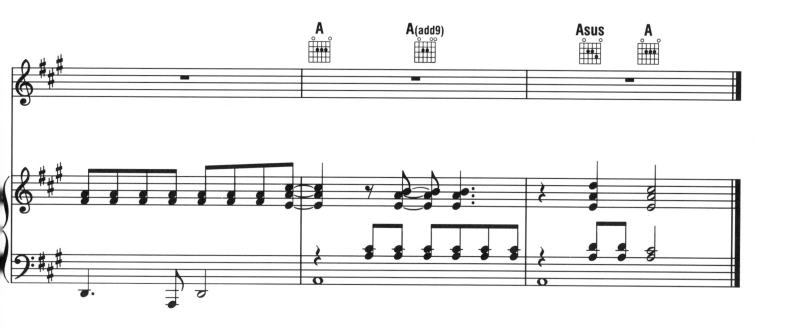

YOU'RE GOING TO LOSE THAT GIRL

Words and Music by
JOHN LENNON and PAUL McCARTNEY

You're gon - na lose that girl. ___ You're gon - na lose ___ that girl. ___

If you don't take her out to - night, ___ she's gon - na

If you don't treat her right my friend, ___ you're gon - na

IT'S ONLY LOVE

Words and Music by
JOHN LENNON and PAUL McCARTNEY

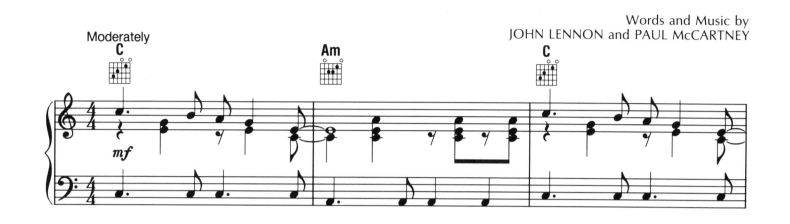

Is it right that I should get high when I see you and go
I get high when I see you go by, my oh my.

fight ev-'ry night?
My oh my.

When you sigh, my, my,
Just the sight of

TICKET TO RIDE

Words and Music by
JOHN LENNON and PAUL McCARTNEY

ACT NATURALLY

Words and Music by
VONIE MORRISON and JOHNNY RUSSELL

ev - er   hit the big - time.

And all I got-ta do is

act nat - 'ral - ly.

We'll

YOU LIKE ME TOO MUCH

Words and Music by
GEORGE HARRISON

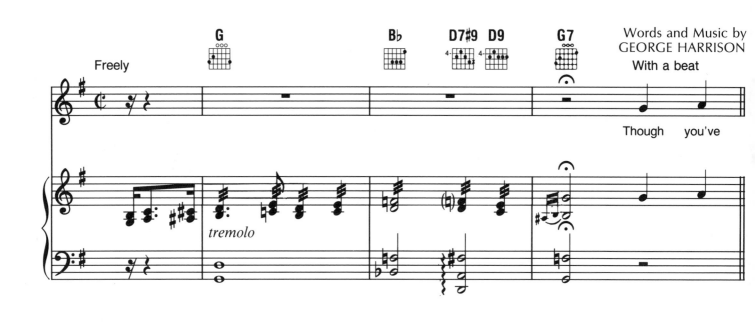

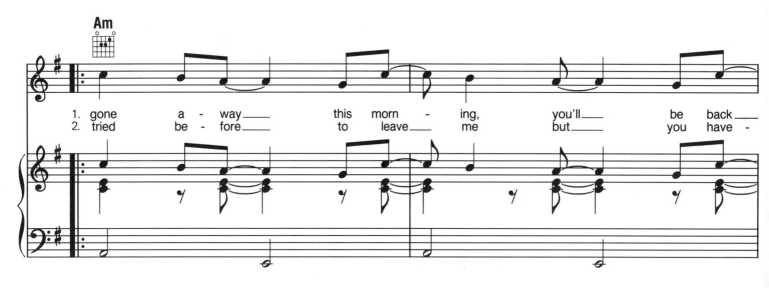

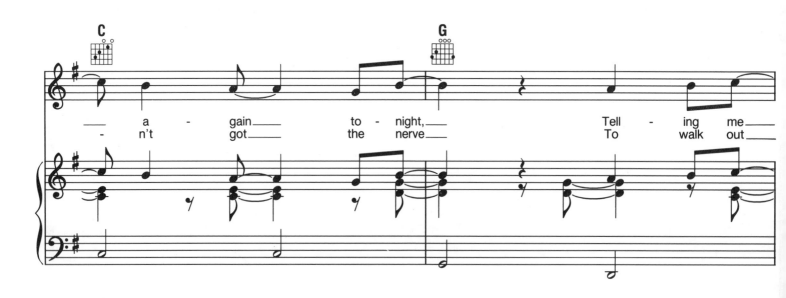

'Cause you like me__ too much__

TELL ME WHAT YOU SEE

Words and Music by
JOHN LENNON and PAUL McCARTNEY

YESTERDAY

Words and Music by JOHN LENNON
and PAUL McCARTNEY

Yes-ter- day,___ all my trou-bles seemed so
Sud-den- ly,___ I'm not half the man___ I

far a - way,___ Now it looks as though___ they're
used to be, There's a sha - dow hang - ing

I'VE JUST SEEN A FACE

Words and Music by
JOHN LENNON and PAUL McCARTNEY

I've just seen a face I can't for-get the time___ or place where we just

D.S. al Coda

CODA

gain.

gain.

Fall - ing, ___ yes, I am fall - ing, ___ And she keeps

call - ing ___ me back a - gain. ___

no chord

gain. ___

DIZZY MISS LIZZIE

Words and Music by
LARRY WILLIAMS

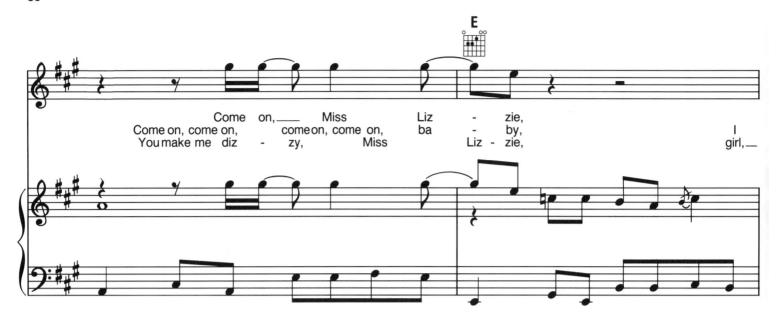

Come on,___ Miss Liz - zie,
Come on, come on, come on, come on, ba - by,
You make me diz - zy, Miss Liz - zie, I girl,___

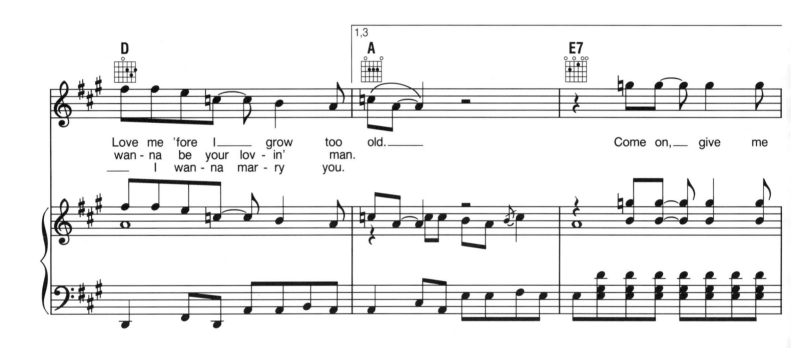

Love me 'fore I___ grow too old.___ Come on,___ give me
wan - na be your lov - in' man.
___ I wan - na mar - ry you.

fe - ver,___ put your lit - tle hand___ in mine.___

DRIVE MY CAR

Words and Music by
JOHN LENNON and PAUL McCARTNEY

Moderately, with a beat

Asked a girl what she
I told the girl what that my
I told that girl I could

want-ed to be.___ She said, "Ba - by, can't you see?___
pros-pects were good,___ And she said "Ba - by, it's un-der-stood.___
start right a - way,___ And she said, "Lis-ten babe, I got some-thing to say.___

I wan-na be fa-mous, a star of the screen,___ But you can do some-thing
Work-ing for pea-nuts is all ver-y fine,___ But I can show you a
I got no car and it's break-ing my heart,___ But I found a driv-er, and

64

NORWEGIAN WOOD
(THIS BIRD HAS FLOWN)

Words and Music by
JOHN LENNON and PAUL McCARTNEY

Moderately

I once had a girl, or should I say she once had me;

(Instrumental)

She showed me her room, is-n't it good Nor-we-gian wood. She
She

asked me to stay and she told me to sit an-y-where, So
told me she worked in the morn-ing and start-ed to laugh, I

NOWHERE MAN

Words and Music by
JOHN LENNON and PAUL McCARTNEY

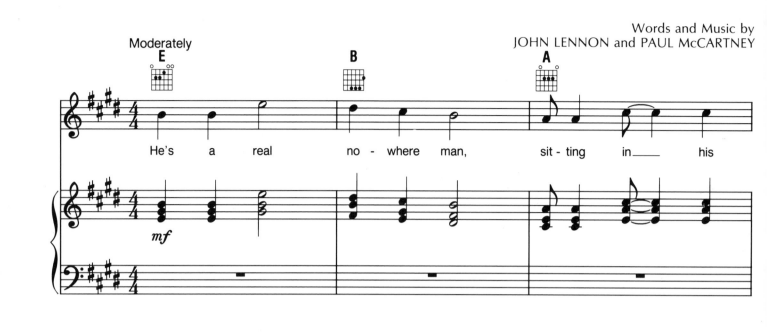

He's a real no-where man, sit-ting in___ his

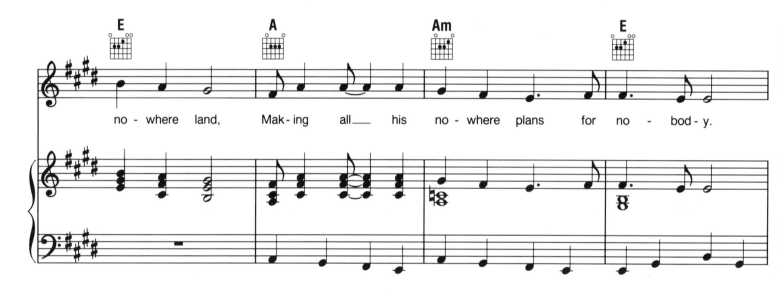

no-where land, Mak-ing all___ his no-where plans for no-bod-y.

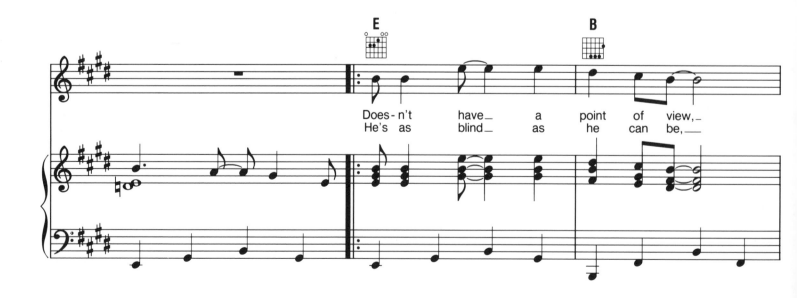

Does-n't have___ a point of view,___
He's as blind___ as he can be,___

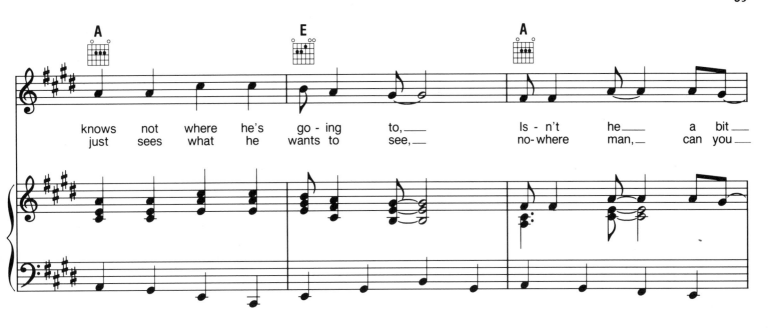

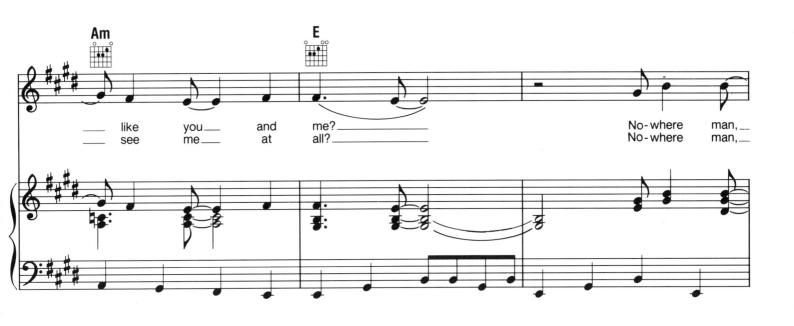

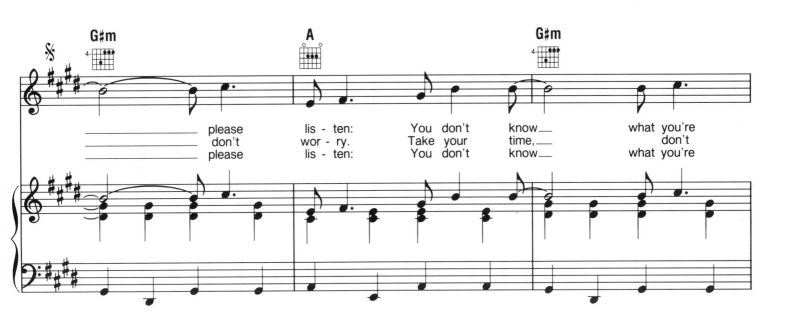

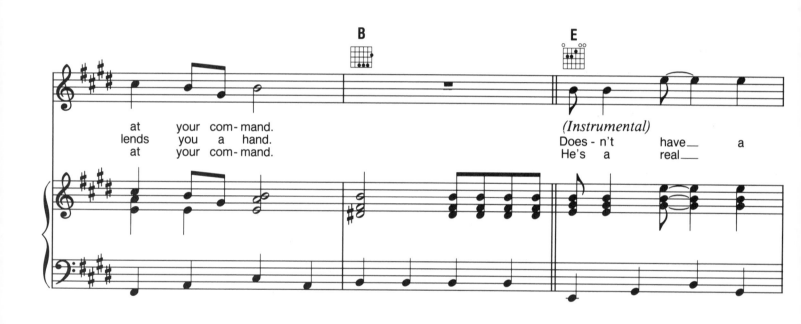

YOU WON'T SEE ME

Words and Music by
JOHN LENNON and PAUL McCARTNEY

THINK FOR YOURSELF

Words and Music by
GEORGE HARRISON

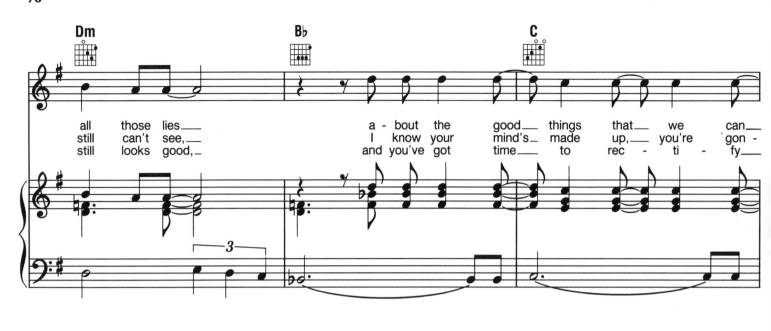

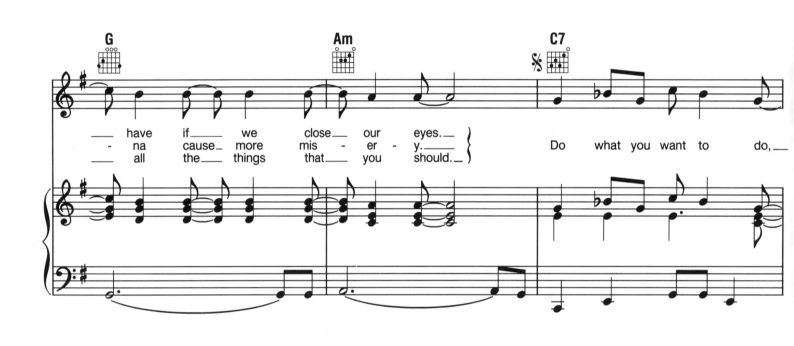

THE WORD

Words and Music by
JOHN LENNON and PAUL McCARTNEY

D7   **G/A**   **A**

heard?_____ The word is "love".
heard?_____ The word is "love".   } It's   so   fine,___ it's
on - ly word is "love".

F/G   **G**   **D7**

sun - shine.___ It's the word   "love."___

1,2,3

Dm   **C**

1. In   the be - gin - ning   I   mis - un - der - stood,___
2. Ev - 'ry - where   I   go   I   hear it   said,___
3. Now that   I know what   I feel must be right,___

MICHELLE

Words and Music by
JOHN LENNON and PAUL McCARTNEY

WHAT GOES ON

Words and Music by JOHN LENNON
PAUL McCARTNEY and RICHARD STARKEY

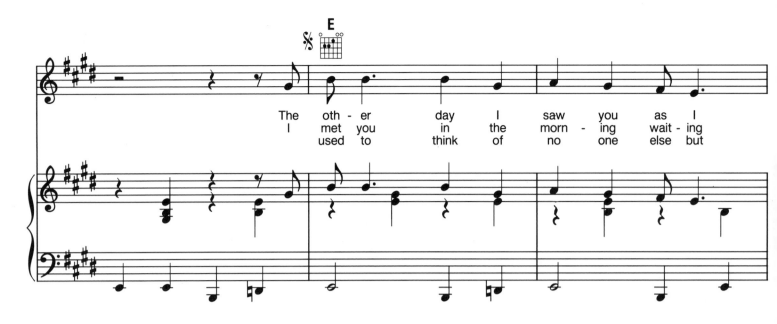

The oth - er day I saw you as I
I met you in the morn - ing wait - ing
used to think of no one else but

walked a - long the road.
for the tides of time.
you were just the same.

But when I saw you with
But now the tides are turn -
You did - n't e - ven think

him I could feel my fu - ture fold.
- ing, I can see that I was blind.
of me as some - one with a name.

It's so
It's so
Did you

GIRL

JOHN LENNON an[...]

Moderately

Cm   G7   Cm

Is there an-y-bod-y going to lis-ten to my
think of all the times I tried so hard to lea[...]
told when she was young that pain would lead to pl[...]

Fm   Eb   G7   Cm   G7

All a-bout the girl who came to stay? She's the kind of girl you want so much it
She will turn to me and start to cry. And she prom-is-es the earth to me and
Did she un-der-stand it when they said That a man must break his back to earn his

Cm   Fm   Cm   To Coda

makes you sor - ry, Still you don't re-gret a sin-gle day.
I be-lieve her, Af-ter all this time I don't know why.   Ah,
day of lei - sure? Will she still be-lieve it when he's dead?

I'M LOOKING THROUGH YOU

Words and Music by

I'm look-ing through____ you,
Your lips are mov -

____ you, where did you go?____
ing, I can - not____ hear.

WAIT

Words and Music by
JOHN LENNON and PAUL McCARTNEY

IF I NEEDED SOMEONE

Words and Music by
GEORGE HARRISON

RUN FOR YOUR LIFE

Words and Music by
JOHN LENNON and PAUL McCARTNEY

IN MY LIFE

Words and Music by
JOHN LENNON and PAUL McCARTNEY

There are plac - es I'll re - mem - ber all my
But of all these friends and lov - ers there is

life,_____ though some have changed.__ Some for - ev - er, not for
no_____ one com - pares with you.__ And these mem - 'ries not lose for their

bet - ter; Some have gone_____ and some re - main.__ All these
mean - ing when I think of__ love as some - thing new.__ Tho' I

116

REVOLVER

TAXMAN

Words and Music by
GEORGE HARRISON

ELEANOR RIGBY

Moderately, with a steady beat

Words and Music by
JOHN LENNON and PAUL McCARTNEY

Ah _____ look at all ____ the lone - ly peo -

- ple! _____

El - ea - nor Rig - by,
Fa - ther Mc Ken - zie
El - ea - nor Rig - by,

picks up the rice___ in the church___ where a wed - ding has been,___
writ - ing the words___ of a ser - mon that no___ one will hear,___
died in the church___ and was bur - ied a - long___ with her name,___

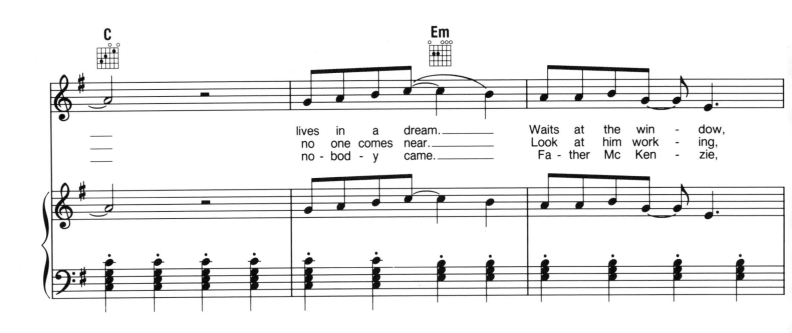

C

Em

___ lives in a dream.___ Waits at the win - dow,
no one comes near.___ Look at him work - ing,
no - bod - y came.___ Fa - ther Mc Ken - zie,

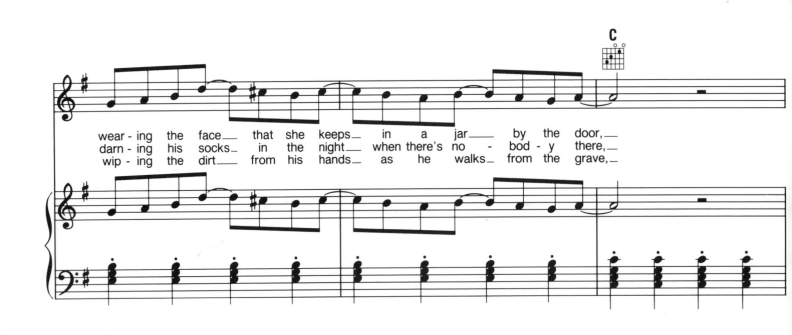

C

wear - ing the face___ that she keeps___ in a jar___ by the door,___
darn - ing his socks___ in the night___ when there's no - bod - y there,___
wip - ing the dirt___ from his hands___ as he walks___ from the grave,___

I'M ONLY SLEEPING

Words and Music by
JOHN LENNON and PAUL McCARTNEY

LOVE YOU TO

Words and Music by
GEORGE HARRISON

Slowly and freely

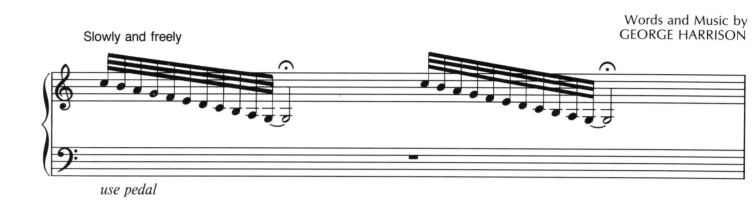

use pedal

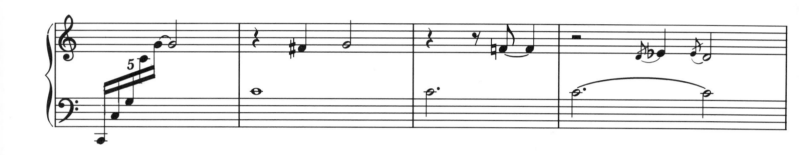

Moderately (strict tempo)

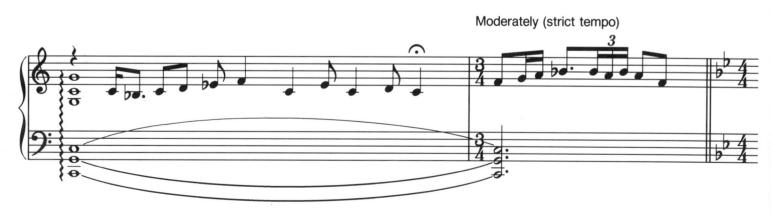

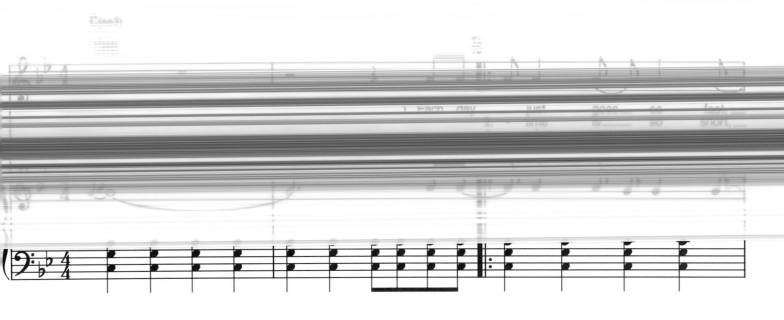

I turn____ a - round,____ it's____ past,____
A new____ one____ can't____ be____ bought.____
Who'll screw____ you____ in____ the____ ground,____

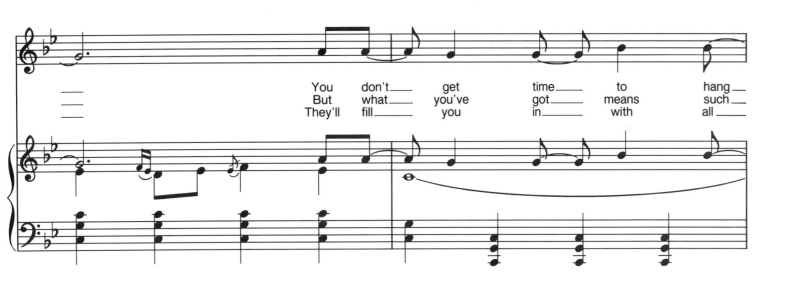

You don't____ get____ time____ to____ hang____
But what____ you've____ got____ means____ such____
They'll fill____ you____ in____ with____ all____

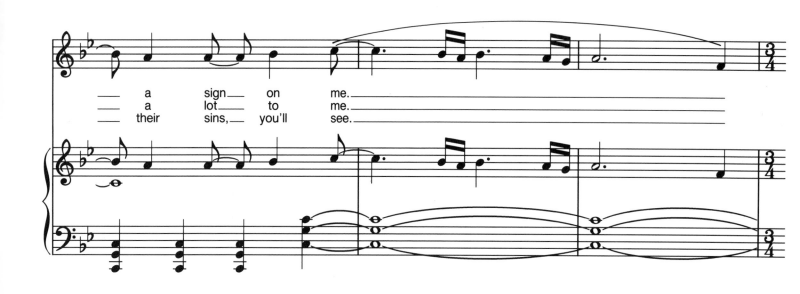

a sign on me.
a lot to me.
their sins, you'll see.

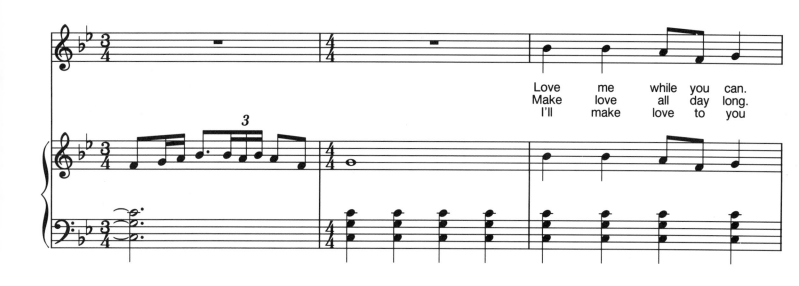

Love me while you can.
Make love all day long.
I'll make love to you

Whole world in a plan.
Make love sing - ing songs.
If you want me to.

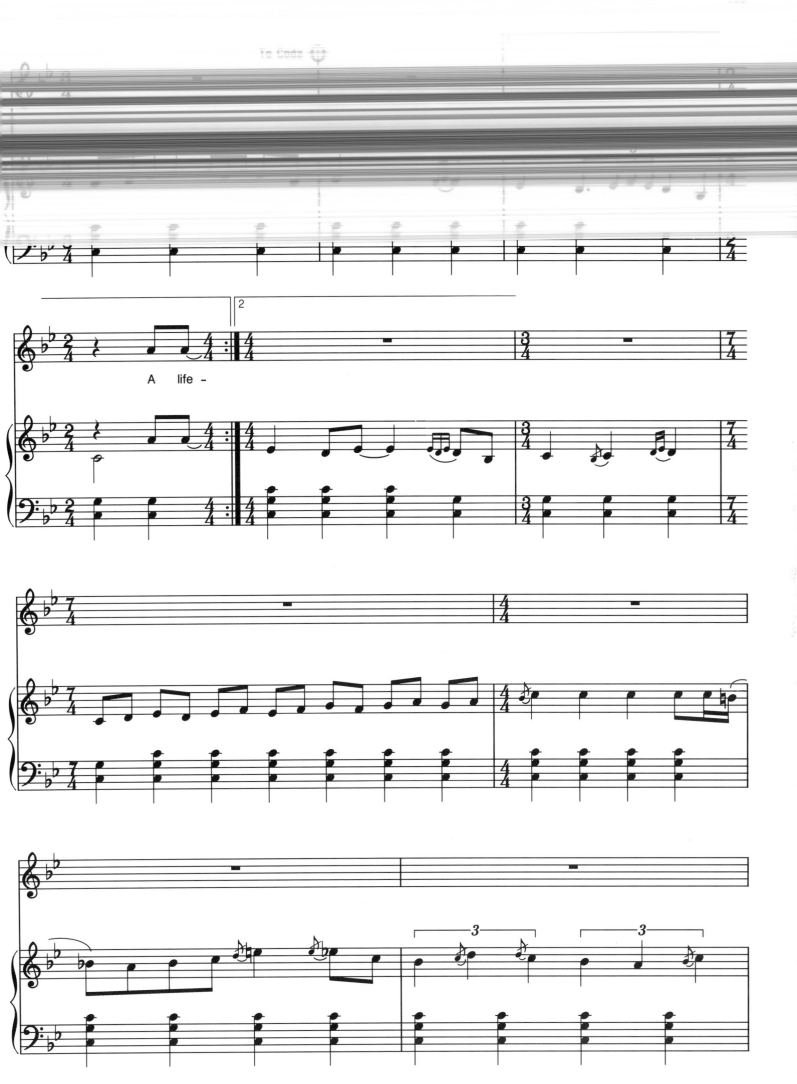

A   life -

134

Make love all day long.

Make love sing-ing songs.

D.S. al Coda

There's peo -

CODA

Faster

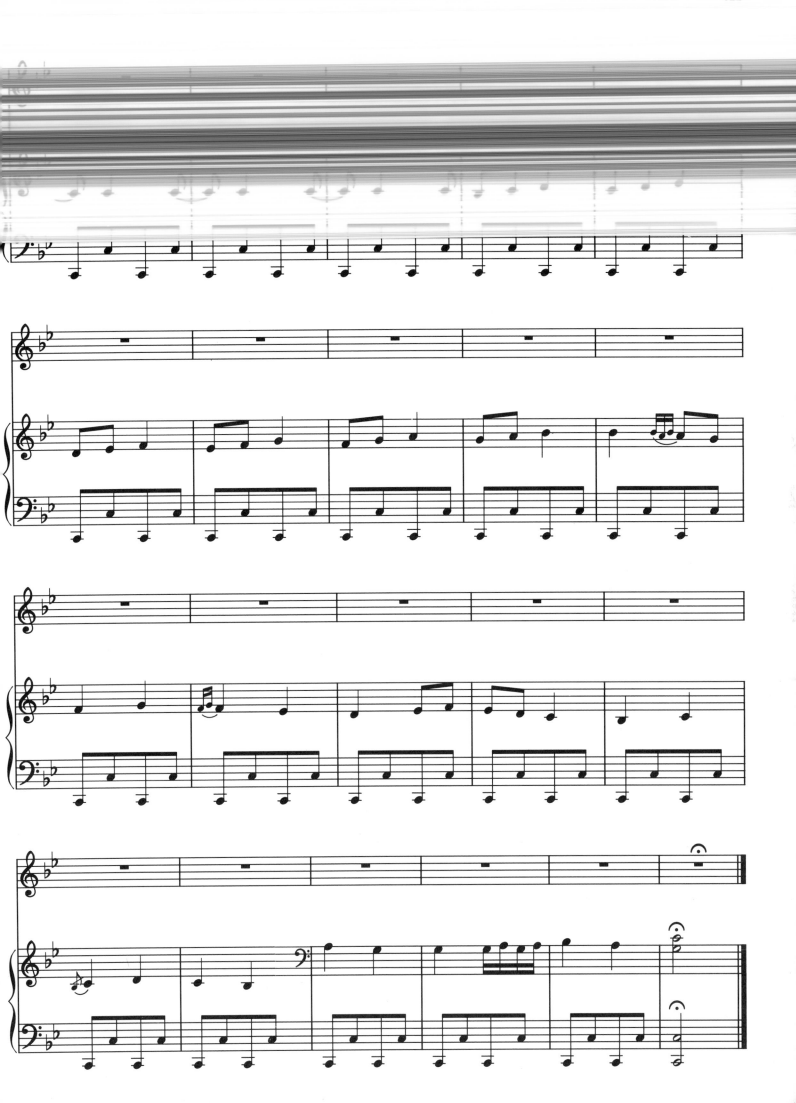

HERE, THERE AND EVERYWHERE

Words and Music by JOHN LENNON
and PAUL McCARTNEY

YELLOW SUBMARINE

Words and Music by
JOHN LENNON and PAUL McCARTNEY

Chorus:

SHE SAID SHE SAID

Words and Music by
JOHN LENNON and PAUL McCARTNEY

ev - 'ry - thing was right." ___ I said, ___

"E - ven though you know what you know,

I know that I'm read - y to leave,

'Cause you're mak - ing me feel ___ like I've

AND YOUR BIRD CAN SING

Words and Music by
JOHN LENNON and PAUL McCARTNEY

Moderately

Tell me that you've got ev-'ry-thing you want,
You say you've seen sev-en won-ders,

and your bird can sing, but you don't get me, ___
and your bird is green, but you can't see me, ___

you don't get me.
you can't see me.

GOOD DAY SUNSHINE

Words and Music by
JOHN LENNON and PAUL McCARTNEY

Good day sun - shine, Good day sun - shine, Good day sun - shine.

I need to
Then we'd

laugh
lie

and when the sun is out
be - neath a shad - y tree,

I've got some - thing I can
I love her and she's

154

FOR NO ONE

DOCTOR ROBERT

Words and Music by
JOHN LENNON and PAUL McCARTNEY

Ring my friend, I said you'd call, Doc-tor
If you're down, he'll pick you up, Doc-tor
My friend works for the Na-tional Health, Doc-tor

Rob-ert.
Rob-ert.
Rob-ert.

Day or night, he'll be
Take a drink from his
Don't pay mon-ey just to

160

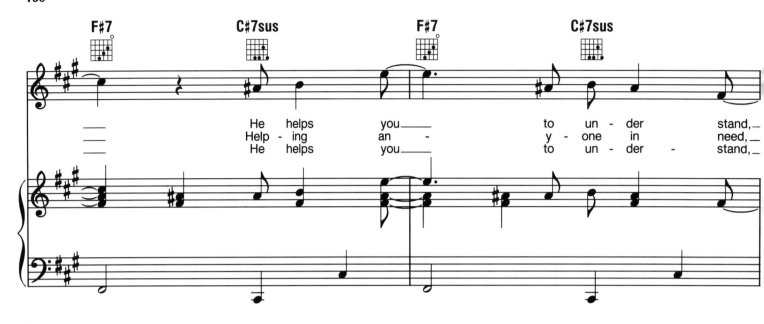

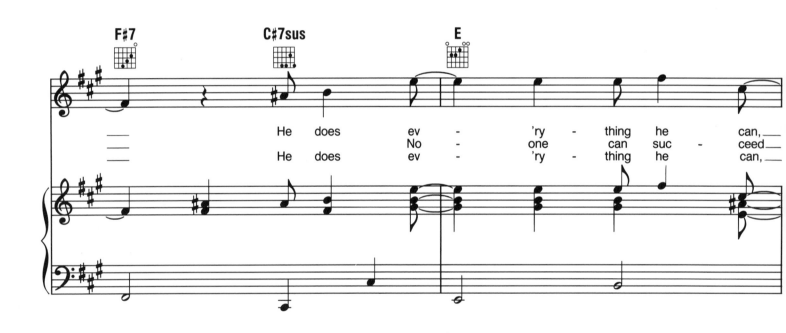

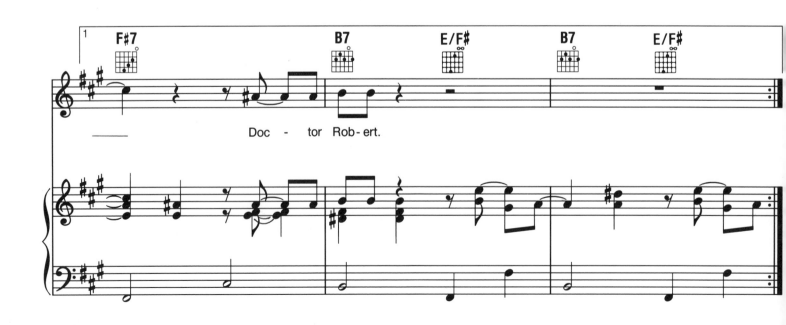

TOMORROW NEVER KNOWS

Words and Music by
JOHN LENNON and PAUL McCARTNEY

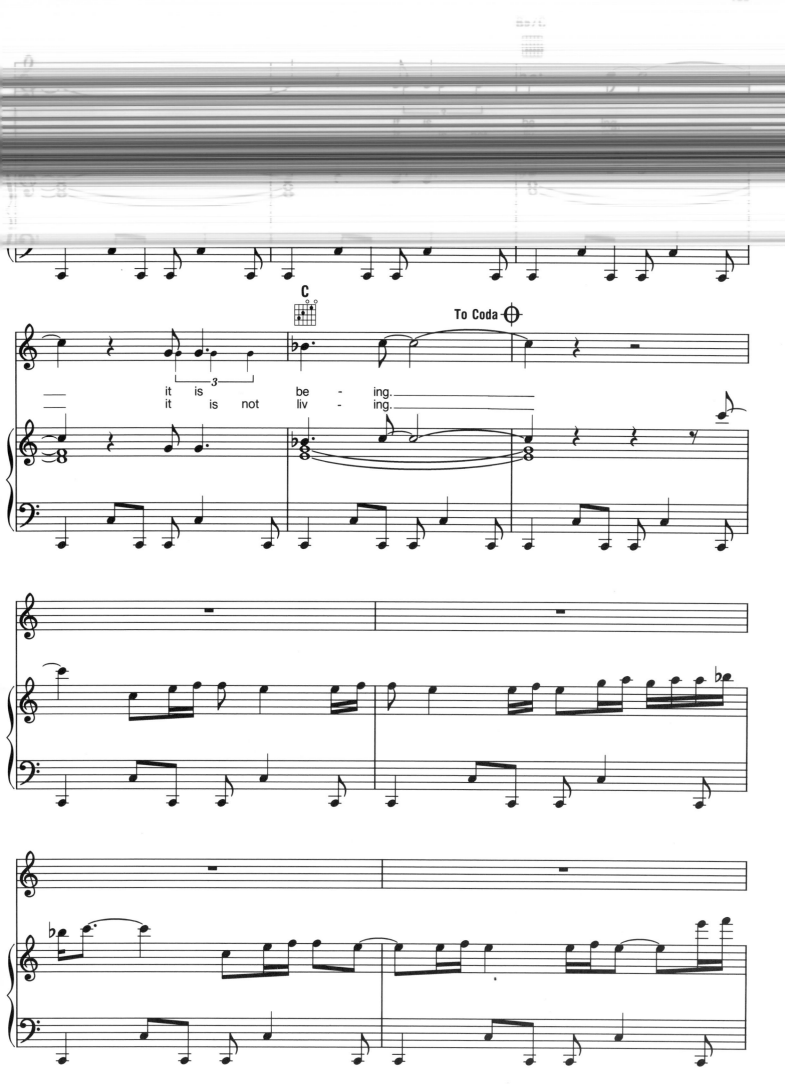

CODA

C

Or play___ the game___ "Ex - is - tence" to the end___

Bb/C

of the be - gin - ning,___

C

Repeat and Fade

of the be - gin - ning,___ of the be -

I WANT TO TELL YOU

Words and Music by
GEORGE HARRISON

I want to tell you, my head is filled with things to say.

GOT TO GET YOU INTO MY LIFE

Words and Music by
JOHN LENNON and PAUL McCARTNEY

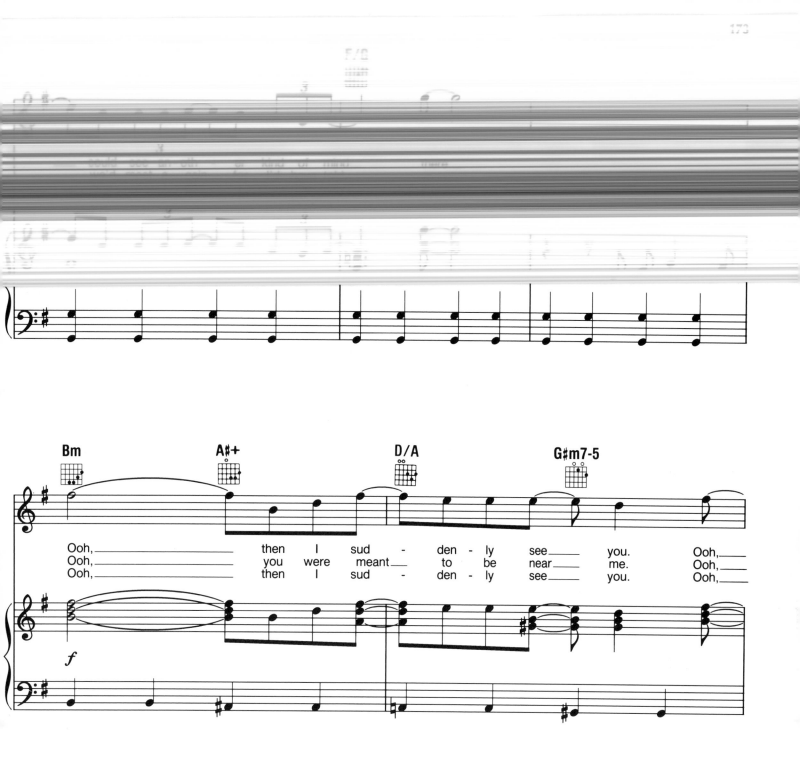

Ooh,_____ then I sud - den - ly see____ you. Ooh,____
Ooh,_____ you were meant____ to be near____ me. Ooh,____
Ooh,_____ then I sud - den - ly see____ you. Ooh,____

_____ did I tell____ you I need____ you ev - 'ry sin - gle
_____ and I want____ you to hear____ me say we'll be to -
_____ did I tell____ you I need____ you ev - 'ry sin - gle

Got to get you in-to my life!___

Repeat and Fade